The Path To Clarity

Create A Life You Love

MICHELLE WORDSWORTH

Copyright © 2019 by Michelle Wordsworth

All rights reserved. No part of this book may be used or reproduced by any means, graphic, electronic, or mechanical, including photocopying, recording, taping, or by any information storage retrieval system, without the written permission of the publisher except in the case of brief quotations embodied in critical articles and reviews.

ISBN: 978-0-6486762-0-1

First Edition 2019 - Paperback

www.michellewordsworth.com

This workbook is dedicated
to you for daring
to dream that anything is possible.

Table of Contents

Introduction ………………………………………………………………..…… 2

Values ………………………………………………………………………..….. 7

Part 1: Values……………………………………………………………..…… 9

Part 2: Wheel Of Life…………………………………………………..…… 15

Part 3: My Power Word …………………………………………………..… 29

Part 4: Soul Purpose & Zone Of Genius……………………………………… 31

Part 5: Your Big Dream ……………………………..………………………… 40

Part 6: Find your Why………………………………..………………………… 44

Part 7: Reframing ……………………….…………………………………..… 51

    Notes……………………………………..……………………………… 61

    Books to Read ………………………………………………………… 65

    Courses & Personal Development I want to do ……………..……………… 67

    12 Month Oracle spread ………………………………….……………… 69

    Quotes & Affirmations to inspire me ……………………………………. 73

    Ideas & Brainstorming ……………………………………………….. 77

    Goals ………………………………………………………………….. 83

    Notes …………………………………………………………………….. 86

The Path To Clarity

Do the work - most people won't!

Give a complex problem to a lazy person and they will find an easy way to get it done.

- Bill Gates

Whether you think you can or you think you can't you are right!

Introduction

About This Workbook

Congratulations on investing in yourself!

You have invested in you to find clarity and turn your vision into reality.

This book has been designed for you to capture all your thoughts and dreams in one place so that you can start manifesting your best life.

The end of 2015 was a big year for me. It was the year that set everything in motion for life-altering changes that were about to happen.

I have used the techniques and questions in this workbook to help me through some of the most challenging times in my career that followed after my internal shift at the end of 2015. I was utterly broken as a person but doing all the mindset and inner work allowed me to gain back control of my life, it helped me realise who I am, and what I wanted in moving forward.

I have been drawn to The Law of Attraction and Manifestation from a young age and have manifested amazing things throughout life. People have said time after time, "Why does everything work out for you?" Or "You always get given things or get what you wish for".

The Path To Clarity

The truth is that I have always set my intentions and also believed that I could have it or achieve it. I never made it a big deal.

The things that worked out the best for me were when I discovered what I wanted and then went on to put things in motion to make it happen, often without even realising it.

I have journaled, used "the cards" played with crystals and even written wishes in tune with the moon phases, you name it, I've done it lol....

It all comes down to clear vision and intention, what you really want and what you are prepared to do to make it happen.

To me, manifestation is bringing to life in a physical form a desire we have within us.

Never underestimate the power of asking yourself what you really want and being crystal clear as to what you desire your life to be.

The magic starts to happen when we identify this, and things will fall into place, the right people will show up, and opportunities will start to present themselves at the right time.

It's up to you what you do with it and the actions you take.

The first part of the workbook is made up of more structured questions designed to help you gain clarity. The second part of the workbook is more for you to use as a journal, notebook and a space for you to jot down any ideas that come to mind so you can keep it all in the one place.

The Path To Clarity

I ask you to answer each question and not skip any. Especially with concern to the questions you want to actually avoid. They are the ones we need to pay even more attention to.

Explore where the questions and answers take you. Have fun, come back and add to them as you think of more things.

You may feel like some of the questions are similar, but I ask you to still answer each question. The more you explore what you want, the clearer you will become, and the more specific you get. You're then more likely to manifest what you want into reality.

Most of all, keep the faith, keep going and if it hasn't happened by when you think it should or want it to, it doesn't mean you have failed, or it won't happen at all.

It just means that it hasn't happened yet and is still on its way to you.

Some things just take a little longer to manifest from thoughts and visions into physical reality.

The best is yet to come and you are just getting started!

The Path To Clarity

Clarity & Action = Results

_____
_____
_____
_____
_____
_____
_____
_____

When you have a vision and know your purpose, anything is possible!

_____
_____
_____
_____
_____
_____
_____
_____

The Path To Clarity

What is happening in your life that has made you want to seek for a change?

_____
_____
_____
_____
_____
_____

What are you most grateful for right now?

_____
_____
_____
_____
_____
_____

Five things that have been amazing in the last 12 months

_____
_____
_____
_____
_____
_____

Values

We are going to start by identifying your most important values.

Values are what our moral compass is tied to. It determines if you are truly living your purpose.

Having values will help you identify what these are, so you can check in to see if you are aligned to what you currently do.

More importantly, this is to ensure that you are in alignment with what you want to create and do as you move forward in life.

Why is this important?

When we know what our values are, we can make decisions based around them.

This can be useful when you are looking for a new job or even a new relationship.

Are your values in alignment with those of the company (or person) and how they operate?

Could it be a deal maker or a deal breaker?

Our values change over time, and what may have been a value you held strong in the past, may no longer be who you are now.

The Path To Clarity

Many people who are unhappy in their work environment or relationships are out of alignment with the company or your own personal values.

There is a mismatch - a disconnect.

When you are no longer in alignment with your values either personally or professionally, this can be an empowering tool to help get you back on track, gain clarity and direction.

The Path To Clarity

Part 1

Values

From the list of values below, pick the most important to you.

Abundance	Finances	Pleasure
Acceptance	Flexibility	Power (Personal power)
Achievement	Flow	Prosperity
Adventure	Freedom	Purpose
Affection	Friendships	Recognition
Ambition	Fun	Relationships
Authenticity	Generosity	Reputation
Balance	Gratitude	Resilience
Bravery	Growth	Respect - self or individual
Calmness	Happiness	Responsibility
Challenger - Self, status Quo	Hard work	Security
Change	Harmony	Self - Love
Collaboration	Health	Self - Reliance

The Path To Clarity

Communication	Honesty	Self-Care
Compassion	Independence	Service
Confidence	Innovation	Simplicity
Connection	Integrity	Social responsibility
Contentment	Intellect	Spirituality
Courage	Intuitiveness	Spontaneity
Creativity	Leadership	Status
Culture	Love	Strength
Curiosity	Loyalty	Structure
Development	Mindfulness	Success
Energy	Money	Teamwork
Ethics	Motivation	Tranquility
Excellence	Open mindedness	Trust
Excitement	Optimism	Wealth
Faith	Originality	Wellbeing
Family	Perseverance	Wisdom
Fearlessness	Personal growth	Worthiness

Feel free to add any additional values not included above to your list.

The Path To Clarity

From the list, pick the 10 most important values to you.

1. _____

2. _____

3. _____

4. _____

5. _____

6. _____

7. _____

8. _____

9. _____

10. _____

Please pick your top 5 most important values.

1. _____

2. _____

3. _____

4. _____

5. _____

The Path To Clarity

How aligned are you to your values?

_____

_____

_____

Now you have picked your top values please give a score out of 10 as to how aligned you currently are to each of them and any ideas or actions you can take to bring you more into alignment to them.

Value	Score out of 10	Ideas /Action
Example: Self-Care	7/10	Schedule more time for me Ensure I am listening more to my body

Part 3
Power Word

How to use a power word:

Use your power word as a pattern interrupter and an anchor to bring you back to the task.

What is a pattern interrupter?

A pattern interrupter is great, it is used to snap you out of a given way of thinking and disrupt your current way of thoughts or actions.

An anchor is something you can use to remember a feeling or a time when you were happy, successful, grateful, taking action, etc.

It is something you use to bring you back into the moment, so you can tap into what you need to keep you motivated and moving forward. To tap back into the feelings that you need to keep positive, motivated and most of all to keep going.

My Power Word

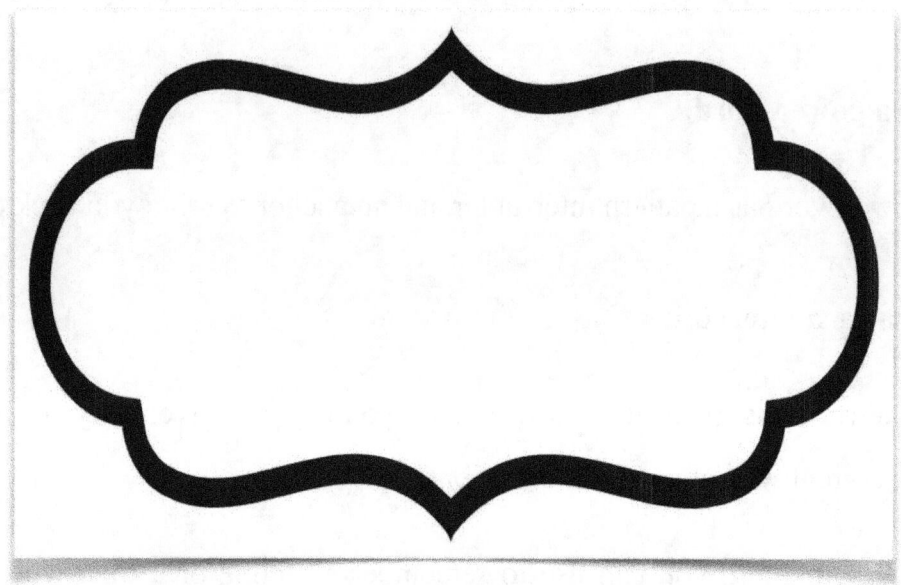

What can I do to help me stay true to this word and focused in accomplishing my end goal?

Part 4

Soul Purpose & Zone Of Genius

Discover what you desire, what brings you alive, what gives you purpose, and what you are good at versus what you are amazing at.

The Big Leap by Gay Hendricks goes through the four different zones and explores where your area of Genius is.

Below is a brief explanation of each level and how I have interpreted and summarised each area.

Zone of Incompetence:

This is where you do not possess the right skill base or mindset. It is something other people do better than you. For example, for me, it would be a doctor or lawyer. I am not good at this, nor do I have a desire to become one or learn about it.

Zone of Competence:

This is where you may be able to do something at a satisfactory level and have an understanding of it. There are other people better at this than you.

An example of this may be an accountant. I can put expenses on a spreadsheet and track incomings and outgoings. However, it would take me a lot more time and effort to do my own taxes, and I would rather leave it to someone who works in the zone like as a genius does. It is something I can do using the basics but not something I am excited about though.

Zone of Excellence:

You can do this at a high level of expertise or skill. Here you have gained a lot of experience and knowledge. It is something you do very well. It may be that there is no-one who can do it quite like you and time seems to pass by relatively quickly or easily. In this area, you are above average and excellent.

For example, in my previous job, I was the only person who performed the role for the whole company. I had lots of knowledge and experience, in fact, I was referred to as the subject matter expert. I found it easy to do while it's still challenging. I was in this role for over 10 years, and it is one I could have continued doing for many more.

However, this was not my passion nor what I really wanted to do even though I was very efficient and successful at it.

Zone of Genius:

Here you are in a natural flow and a state of excitement. You feel energised and you are acting with purpose. This is something you could see yourself doing forever, even if you were not being paid.

No one can do the task like you and time flies while you are absorbed in it.

The Path To Clarity

Most people are stuck in the zone of competence or excellence and think this is where they have to stay. They have job security, so why rock the boat or give up a sure thing like a regular pay-check?

Where we come alive is when we are in our zone of genius.

We will be exploring exercises to help you reveal what your zone of genius is.

Discovering your zone of genius uncovers what drives you and is bigger than you.

It is what lies within us, which motivates and inspires us to take action.

It gives us purpose and meaning behind what we do and can be the reason for us to get out of bed in the morning.

When we have such a drive and a yearning it is often all we need to inspire us to take action to create change in our life - big or small.

One small change may be a catalyst to turn your life around. It keeps you moving towards what lights you up even on the most challenging of days because we have the inner desire and purpose within us.

When we discover what our zone of genius is it unlocks our potential and what we have kept hidden inside - our souls purpose.

You may find throughout these exercises that you have multiple passions and areas of genius, which is great. This is a space for you to discover and record them.

The Path To Clarity

You can work through and see which one has the strongest pull for you right now and you can then return and explore others identified on your list.

As you proceed, make sure not to limit your thinking to one area.

Use this exercise to discover what you are excellent in versus what you are a genius at.

Are they in alignment with your personal values?

How does this fit in with your Wheel of Life?

As you go through and answer each question, take time and allow yourself to....

Create uninterrupted time for yourself

Write down as much as you can for each answer.

Let it flow naturally - if it isn't, move on and return to it.

Think about what your friends and family comment that you are good at.

Ask friends and family to provide you with feedback. It may help you to think of things which are obvious but forgotten about.

_____
_____
_____
_____
_____

The Path To Clarity

I am good at…

_____

_____

_____

_____

_____

_____

What do I want more of in my life? (Including how I want to feel)

_____

_____

_____

_____

_____

_____

I love doing…

_____

_____

_____

_____

_____

_____

The Path To Clarity

Every day I think about…

_____

_____

_____

_____

_____

_____

New interests I would like to explore are:

_____

_____

_____

_____

_____

_____

People I want to spend more time around - this can be an idea of a type of person or someone specific.

_____

_____

_____

_____

_____

_____

The Path To Clarity

A secret dream I would love to fulfill is:

_____
_____
_____
_____
_____
_____

Referring to the above answers, identify recurring themes and make a list in the space below. Hint - this may fall into your zone of genius.

_____
_____
_____
_____
_____
_____

List anything else you have not already captured.

_____
_____
_____
_____
_____
_____

The Path To Clarity

What could be regarded as more of a hobby rather than your purpose/zone of genius?

_____
_____
_____
_____
_____

From the above lists, are there any common threads or themes? Can they link to each other in any way?

_____
_____
_____
_____
_____

Where the three overlap = Your Zone Of Genius

If you are still having trouble pinpointing your zone of genius, think about the following:

Brainstorm

Your purpose and zone of genius could be for yourself or a new source of income, so think bigger than your purpose being for you. It could be a gift for you to share or help others.

Make a list of anything which comes to mind, don't overthink, just let it flow.

What could I do to start incorporating my identified purpose and zone of genius into my life, create income or, start a new business from my passion?

Part 5

Your Big Dream

This is your time to dream big and think about what exactly you really want and what your BIG VISION looks like.

What if you could decide how you wanted life to work for you. How would that look?

When you know what your big vision or dream is, you have a destination.

You can then use this to work backwards and brainstorm all the steps and options you may need to act on or consider to make it happen.

When you have a plan, everything seems to be a lot more believable and achievable.

You can then use this to break it down into smaller steps so as not to be overwhelmed.

This is why having a big dream or a vision is so important.

It is much easier when you know where you are going.

It helps remove fears because we can plan and have contingencies in place to rule out the fears.

This gives us the ability to move forward.

Use the 'Ideal Day Visualisation' available at michellewordsworth.com/ideal-day before answering the questions below. This will be useful to help expand your answers.

When thinking about your ideal day - your big vision dream, take into account what has come up for you so far with your wheel of life and values.

What does your ideal life look like?

Have fun exploring this, it is a space for you to really dream and write anything that occurs to you, no matter how big or unrealistic it seems. There are no rules or limitations. This is a place for you to list them all.

Use the following questions as prompts to help you map out your Big Dream and Vision

Think about:

What lights you up and makes you come alive?

What would you like to have in life? Don't be shy write it down!

What invigorates you?

What is it that fills your dreams at night?

What is it you would happily do even if you weren't getting paid?

What would you like to create?

What would you do if you had all the money in the world?

What would you like to be?

What would you like to be remembered for?

If you had no limitations, what would you do?

Big Vision - Ideal Life

Part 6

Find your Why

Now that you have explored your dreams and what your Ideal life is, we are going to explore the "WHY" behind what you want. This is the marker to confirm how much you really want the things you desire.

When you discover and become clear on this, it will change your life!

It will bring in powerful shifts and give you purpose behind each step you take towards your goal.

In this section, you will incorporate what you have uncovered from the previous exercises, especially where you explored your big dream.

Write a list of all the things you identified you wanted from the previous sections. Feel free to add on any more you think of as well. Pick the top thing you would like to focus on as being the most important.

Below is space for you to explore this one thing.

Once you have done this, ask yourself the following questions. Space has been provided, for you to come up with more of your own ideas and would like to explore further.

There is also a section to record any reasons or thoughts which arise as to why what you want won't work. We will be exploring this later, but it is good to jot anything that does pop up here so you can refer to and expand on it later.

This gives you the ability to identify and to see if they are really true or not and find ways through, around or over them.

Once you have completed this, go through and see if there are any common threads that appear and note any "aha" moments. By doing this exercise, it can offer amazing insights.

The idea of these questions is to find out why and how it benefits you, but also why having these things can benefit others by looking at the bigger picture.

In identifying this, it will enable us to give more meaning and purpose behind why we want what we want and can have what we desire, and so we are more likely to achieve it.

Enjoy the process and don't overanalyse – but allow yourself to write down anything that comes to mind.

What I Want

The Path To Clarity

Why do I want this?

_____
_____
_____
_____
_____
_____
_____
_____
_____

What are the benefits to me having this and why is it important for me to have?

_____
_____
_____
_____
_____
_____
_____
_____
_____

The Path To Clarity

How will I feel when I have it?

_____
_____
_____
_____
_____

Who does it serve and why does it serve others if I have this?

_____
_____
_____
_____
_____

How does it change my life and the life of others?

_____
_____
_____
_____
_____
_____

The Path To Clarity

By having this, how does it affect those around me and the world in general in a positive way? - Think about the ripple effect.

_____
_____
_____
_____
_____
_____

What are all the reasons why it won't work? - We will be exploring this, so do well to write down anything that pops into your head here, and we will come back to it I promise.

_____
_____
_____
_____
_____
_____

The Path To Clarity

Additional space for more questions you come up with and would like to explore.

Part 7

Reframing

What we will do now is to flip our fears and negative thoughts into more positive statements.

This is where we take all the reasons identified as to why we think we can't have whatever it is we want and ask the following questions for each reason:

Are the reasons I have identified as to why I can't have this really true?

If you have answered yes - Ask yourself again 'Is this ultimately true?"

Are the reasons you have identified relevant right now? - They could be something you are using as an excuse that has no impact right now or ever. And even if it does, it is so far down the track by the time it becomes an issue, you will be more than likely to have the relevant tools, knowledge, resources and people to assist you with it.

For example, some people use the excuse that if they earn more they have to pay more taxes so they would rather earn less, so they pay less tax. Who does this really serve?

Or, people associate having more money with the fear of people taking advantage of them. When you have more money, you can put in place steps to prevent this from happening and pay someone if needed to help you do this.

Everything has a way around it, a way through, a way over and can be worked out if you want it badly enough. Otherwise, they end up just being excuses we hide behind because we really didn't want it badly enough to begin with.

This leads to the next question. For each excuse or reason as to why it might not work - what are ways to overcome and bridge these gaps between where you are now and where you want to be?

Once you have completed this in the space below, use the following page to list all the reasons why you have said it won't work and write in the opposite column a new empowering statement as to why it will work.

Example:
Negative - I don't know enough to teach on this subject yet…
Positive - I am constantly gaining more knowledge and sharing as I learn.

The Path To Clarity

Why I believe it won't work	Reframe To Positive

The Path To Clarity

Now you are clear on what you want and have silenced any self-sabotaging talk you will want to know what to do next.

This is where you can start to plan out your next steps.

Go back and revisit the ideas you wrote down when you explored what you can do to start closing the gaps from where you are now to where you want to be.

Pick something easy to start with, so you gain momentum and know you can achieve it.

Feel free to download my free Goal Planner at michellelwordsworth.com/planner

What you want to do is create a goal/wish/dream - whatever you prefer to call it and then set a timeframe for when you want to have achieved it.

The next step is to create little action steps working backward from this goal to where you currently are.

To set yourself up for the best success, keep in mind the following.

Make your goal something you believe you can achieve but is just outside your current reach at the moment (let's face it, if it wasn't then you would have accomplished it already).

Use the Wheel of Life exercise to see which area of your life is most important right now and what you want to focus on the most.

By using the 'Big Vision', you can start to imagine what this could look like for you.

Get as specific as you can.

The Path To Clarity

Make sure you put in place ways to track your progress so you can see that it is attainable and monitor your progress.

This will help you stay on track.

Make sure the steps you take each day, contributes something no matter how small it is to move you closer to your goals and what you want to manifest into your life.

Never be afraid to ask.

Always believe you are worthy.

Begin imagining yourself as though you have already reached your goal. Feel the feeling as though it is already yours now!

Make sure you are taking the actions required.

Lastly, be open and ready to receive all the amazing things coming into your life!

The following pages are for you to daydream and brainstorm, make notes, create your plan and have some fun!

My Big Dreams

My Big Dreams

My Big Dreams

My Big Dreams

The Path To Clarity

My Big Dreams

The Path To Clarity

Notes

The Path To Clarity

Notes

Notes

The Path To Clarity

<u>Notes</u>

The Path To Clarity

Books to Read

The Path To Clarity

Books to Read

Courses & Personal Development I want to do

Courses & Personal Development I want to do

The Path To Clarity

12 Month Oracle spread

Use your favourite deck or positive affirmations to create a 12 month spread to see what strengths you can fall into to motivate and keep you on track. Start by taking 1 as either January or the month you are in right now. Follow around for the 12 months and then card 13 is an overall theme of the year.

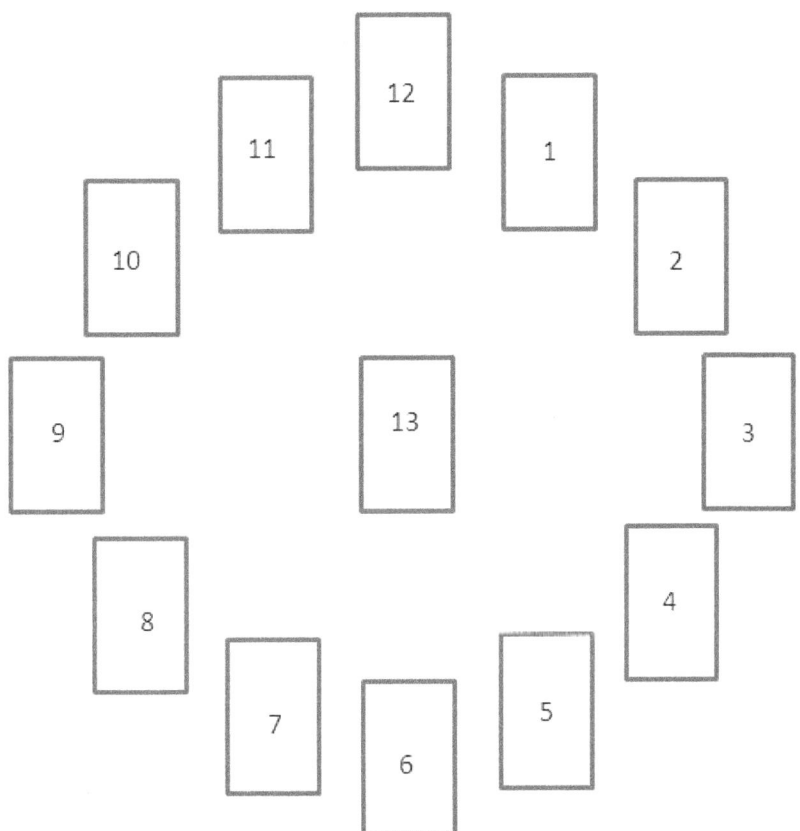

The Path To Clarity

12 Month Oracle spread

Notes

The Path To Clarity

Notes

Quotes & Affirmations to inspire me

The Path To Clarity

Quotes & Affirmations to inspire me

Quotes & Affirmations to inspire me

The Path To Clarity

Quotes & Affirmations to inspire me

Ideas & Brainstorming

Ideas & Brainstorming

Ideas & Brainstorming

Ideas & Brainstorming

Ideas & Brainstorming

Ideas & Brainstorming

Goals

The Path To Clarity

Goals

The Path To Clarity

Goals

Notes

Notes

Notes

The Path To Clarity

Notes

The Path To Clarity

Notes

Notes

The Path To Clarity

Notes

The Path To Clarity

<u>Notes</u>

Notes

Notes

Final Words

Dream Big and create a life you love!

If you want something bad enough, you will find ways to make it happen.

The most important thing is to have fun and follow your heart!

If you want more of this and to join women like yourself in creating and manifesting your dream life, check out your perfect next step here:

Visit: michellewordsworth.com

To learn more on the Law of Attraction and Manifestation, Mindset and Personal Development, you can work with me one on one, in group programs, live events or through my online courses.

Visit: michellelwordsworth.com

Follow me on Facebook at:
https://www.facebook.com/michellewordsworthcom

Follow me on Instagram at:
https://www.instagram.com/michellewordsworthcom/

Follow me on Pinterest at:
https://www.pinterest.com.au/michellewordsworth/

www.ingramcontent.com/pod-product-compliance
Lightning Source LLC
Chambersburg PA
CBHW082244300426
44110CB00036B/2439